Baby Shower Games

Play-Sheets, Instructions, and Helpful Tips for the Hostess

CHRONICLE BOOKS
SAN FRANCISCO

Text © 2007 Chronicle Books LLC
Illustrations © 2007 Maybelle Imasa-Stukuls

All rights reserved. No part of this book may be reproduced
in any form without written permission from the publisher.

ISBN 0-8118-5677-1
Text by *Sharron Wood*
Design by *Kristen Hewitt*
Calligraphy & Illustrations by *Maybelle Imasa-Stukuls*
Typeset in Bodoni
Manufactured in China

Chronicle Books endeavors to use environmentally responsible
paper in its gift and stationery products.

Distributed in Canada by
Raincoast Books
9050 Shaughnessy Street
Vancouver, B.C. V6P 6E5

10 9 8 7 6 5 4 3 2 1

Chronicle Books LLC
680 Second Street
San Francisco, CA 94107
www.chroniclebooks.com

Introduction

Organizing a baby shower is one of the happiest hostessing occasions of all:
What could be better than celebrating a new life and the mom who is bringing
it into being? Because everyone at the event will be thrilled for the guest of
honor, you can count on a festive atmosphere, but playing a few well-chosen
games can still go a long way toward ensuring that everyone has a good time,
and that those who are not yet acquainted get to know more about each other—
or about the mother-to-be.

Whether you're planning a casual coed backyard barbecue or an intimate tea
for the mother-to-be's closest girlfriends, you'll find games here that suit the
occasion. A small gathering of good friends might prefer the silliness of games
like "Baby Shower Bingo," while a more diverse group of women of different
generations might prefer more traditional games like "Who Knows Mommy
Best?" The eight ready-to-play games will free you up to attend to all the other
pressing party planning details, from choosing the location and invitations
to decorating and preparing food and drinks. There are fifteen play-sheets
included for each game; if your party is larger, you can easily photocopy more
sheets ahead of time, or purchase an extra game pad.

The final Gift Tracker pages can be used to keep a record of the gifts mom
receives and the name of the gift giver. If you assign a guest sitting next to the
mom-to-be the job of recording this information, she will surely appreciate
having it when she sits down to write her thank-you notes.

Hosting the Games

If I Were a Mom . . .
Have each guest fill in their "If I Were a Mom" game sheet. Collect the
sheets and redistribute them randomly. Each guest reads the sheet that
has been handed to her while everyone else tries to guess who filled
it out. The guest who guesses correctly most consistently is awarded a
prize, but the real goal of the game is to break the ice and get everyone
acquainted.

Who Knows Mommy Best?

This game gives everyone a chance to learn a bit more about the guest of honor. After everyone completes the quiz, ask the mom-to-be to reveal her answers so everyone can tally up their score. For an extra bit of fun, have the baby's father complete the quiz in advance and compare how he did with the guests. Does he know Mommy as well as her mother or her best friend?

Baby Shower Bingo

Before the mom-to-be starts unwrapping her presents, have guests fill out their bingo cards with the names of the gifts they expect her to receive. As players get very close to scoring a "bingo," you might be surprised that everyone has an opinion about which gift mom should open next. The first guest to score "bingo" wins. If no one scores a bingo, give the prize to the person with the most Xs on their card.

Mystery Meats and Other Baby Foods

Prior to the party, purchase ten different types of baby food and cover each label with a strip of paper. Each guest will be handed a spoon and asked to taste from each jar and record their guess as to what its contents are. Be sure to buy a wide variety of foods: applesauce and pureed carrots are easy to identify, while items like turkey or cauliflower will stump almost everyone. The player with the highest number of correct guesses wins.

It's All Relative

You'll need a watch with a second-timer for this fast-paced brainteaser. Inform your guests that they will have two minutes to complete the quiz and then hand out the game sheets facedown. Since the answers to almost all these questions can be figured out if guests are given enough time, the two-minute time limit will frazzle and amuse the players. To increase the pressure, be sure to give them a warning when they have only 30 seconds left. The highest number of correct answers wins. The answers to this game appear on the inside back cover of this book.

TV Tots

This breezy trivia game tests your guests' knowledge of children's television. Drawing from a roster of modern and classic kids' TV shows, your guests will have two minutes to match the tot with the show he or she appears on. If you like, you can divide your guests into teams to increase

the excitement. The answers to this game appear on the inside back cover of this book.

Animal Babies

See whether your guests know their pups from their cubs in this fill-in-the-blanks test. The players will have two minutes to pair up the list of adult animal names with their baby counterparts. If you like, you can divide your guests into teams to increase the excitement. The answers to this game appear on the inside back cover of this book.

Newborn Know-How

Gauge your guests' knowledge of baby facts and trivia with this quiz. Your guests will have three minutes to answer the 10 questions and test their baby IQ. If you like, you can divide your guests into teams to increase the excitement. The answers to this game appear on the inside back cover of this book.

Prizes

If you want your guests to play these games with gusto, award prizes to the winners. Prizes don't need to be pricey, but they should reflect the style of the guests as much as possible. You know best whether your guests are likely to appreciate little luxuries like scented candles, or bath salts, or whether a gift certificate from an online bookseller or a local café might be more their style. If many of the guests are parents of young children themselves, picture frames and small photo albums are sure to be well received. Edible gifts are almost always appreciated, whether it's an elegant little box of chocolates, some gourmet coffee or tea, or homemade cookies in the shape of a baby bottle or rubber ducky. Small potted plants, packets of seeds for kitchen herbs, or even tiny saplings that guests can take home and plant will serve as a reminder of the baby's birth for a long time to come.

Whatever the prize, take a few moments to package it prettily. A bit of ribbon or a little sprig of fresh flowers makes any package special. Finally, consider that you can make the party decorations do double duty. If you've arranged flowers to brighten up the party location, dole them out to the winning guests on their way out.

If I Were a Mom . . .

*Fill in the blanks in the following sentences, taking care
not to let the other guests see your answers. When you're done,
hand your answer sheet to the hostess.*

1. My favorite thing about babies is ....
....

2. If my baby woke me up four times every night, I would ....
....

3. The first solid food I would feed my baby is ....

4. My baby's first word would probably be ....

5. If I needed a break from caring for the baby, I would call ....

6. My ideal number of children would be ....

7. The one thing I would always do for my baby is ....
....

8. The one thing I would never do to my baby is ....
....

9. The problem with today's parents is ....
....

10. When I was a baby I, ...
....

If I Were a Mom . . .

*Fill in the blanks in the following sentences, taking care
not to let the other guests see your answers. When you're done,
hand your answer sheet to the hostess.*

1. My favorite thing about babies is ....
....

2. If my baby woke me up four times every night, I would ....
....

3. The first solid food I would feed my baby is ....

4. My baby's first word would probably be ....

5. If I needed a break from caring for the baby, I would call ....

6. My ideal number of children would be ....

7. The one thing I would always do for my baby is ....
....

8. The one thing I would never do to my baby is ....
....

9. The problem with today's parents is ....
....

10. When I was a baby I, ...
....

If I Were a Mom . . .

*Fill in the blanks in the following sentences, taking care
not to let the other guests see your answers. When you're done,
hand your answer sheet to the hostess.*

1. My favorite thing about babies is ....
....

2. If my baby woke me up four times every night, I would ....
....

3. The first solid food I would feed my baby is ....

4. My baby's first word would probably be ....

5. If I needed a break from caring for the baby, I would call ....

6. My ideal number of children would be ....

7. The one thing I would always do for my baby is ....
....

8. The one thing I would never do to my baby is ....
....

9. The problem with today's parents is ....
....

10. When I was a baby I, ...
....

If I Were a Mom . . .

*Fill in the blanks in the following sentences, taking care
not to let the other guests see your answers. When you're done,
hand your answer sheet to the hostess.*

1. My favorite thing about babies is ....
....

2. If my baby woke me up four times every night, I would ....
....

3. The first solid food I would feed my baby is ....

4. My baby's first word would probably be ....

5. If I needed a break from caring for the baby, I would call ....

6. My ideal number of children would be ....

7. The one thing I would always do for my baby is ....
....

8. The one thing I would never do to my baby is ....
....

9. The problem with today's parents is ....
....

10. When I was a baby I, ...
....

If I Were a Mom . . .

Fill in the blanks in the following sentences, taking care
not to let the other guests see your answers. When you're done,
hand your answer sheet to the hostess.

1. My favorite thing about babies is ....

   ....

2. If my baby woke me up four times every night, I would ....

   ....

3. The first solid food I would feed my baby is ....

4. My baby's first word would probably be ....

5. If I needed a break from caring for the baby, I would call ....

6. My ideal number of children would be ....

7. The one thing I would always do for my baby is ....

   ....

8. The one thing I would never do to my baby is ....

   ....

9. The problem with today's parents is ....

   ....

10. When I was a baby I, ...

    ....

If I Were a Mom . . .

*Fill in the blanks in the following sentences, taking care
not to let the other guests see your answers. When you're done,
hand your answer sheet to the hostess.*

1. My favorite thing about babies is ....

    ....

2. If my baby woke me up four times every night, I would ....

    ....

3. The first solid food I would feed my baby is ....

4. My baby's first word would probably be ....

5. If I needed a break from caring for the baby, I would call ....

6. My ideal number of children would be ....

7. The one thing I would always do for my baby is ....

    ....

8. The one thing I would never do to my baby is ....

    ....

9. The problem with today's parents is ....

    ....

10. When I was a baby I, ...

    ....

If I Were a Mom . . .

*Fill in the blanks in the following sentences, taking care
not to let the other guests see your answers. When you're done,
hand your answer sheet to the hostess.*

1. My favorite thing about babies is ....

....

2. If my baby woke me up four times every night, I would ....

....

3. The first solid food I would feed my baby is ....

4. My baby's first word would probably be ....

5. If I needed a break from caring for the baby, I would call ....

6. My ideal number of children would be ....

7. The one thing I would always do for my baby is ....

....

8. The one thing I would never do to my baby is ....

....

9. The problem with today's parents is ....

....

10. When I was a baby I, ...

....

If I Were a Mom . . .

*Fill in the blanks in the following sentences, taking care
not to let the other guests see your answers. When you're done,
hand your answer sheet to the hostess.*

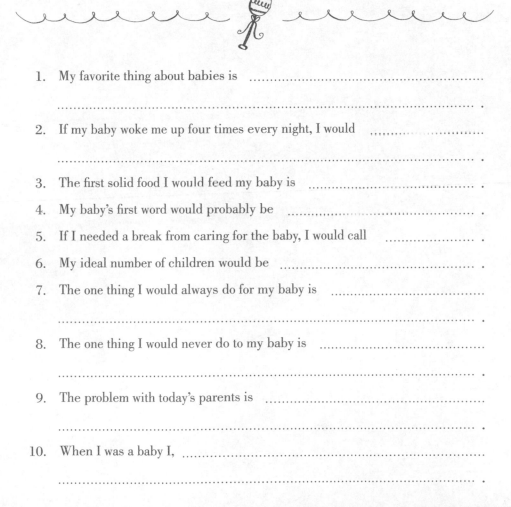

1. My favorite thing about babies is ....

   ....

2. If my baby woke me up four times every night, I would ....

   ....

3. The first solid food I would feed my baby is ....

4. My baby's first word would probably be ....

5. If I needed a break from caring for the baby, I would call ....

6. My ideal number of children would be ....

7. The one thing I would always do for my baby is ....

   ....

8. The one thing I would never do to my baby is ....

   ....

9. The problem with today's parents is ....

   ....

10. When I was a baby I, ...

    ....

If I Were a Mom . . .

*Fill in the blanks in the following sentences, taking care
not to let the other guests see your answers. When you're done,
hand your answer sheet to the hostess.*

1. My favorite thing about babies is ....
   ....

2. If my baby woke me up four times every night, I would ....
   ....

3. The first solid food I would feed my baby is ....

4. My baby's first word would probably be ....

5. If I needed a break from caring for the baby, I would call ....

6. My ideal number of children would be ....

7. The one thing I would always do for my baby is ....
   ....

8. The one thing I would never do to my baby is ....
   ....

9. The problem with today's parents is ....
   ....

10. When I was a baby I, ...
    ....

If I Were a Mom . . .

*Fill in the blanks in the following sentences, taking care
not to let the other guests see your answers. When you're done,
hand your answer sheet to the hostess.*

1. My favorite thing about babies is ....
....

2. If my baby woke me up four times every night, I would ....
....

3. The first solid food I would feed my baby is ....

4. My baby's first word would probably be ....

5. If I needed a break from caring for the baby, I would call ....

6. My ideal number of children would be ....

7. The one thing I would always do for my baby is ....
....

8. The one thing I would never do to my baby is ....
....

9. The problem with today's parents is ....
....

10. When I was a baby I, ...
....

If I Were a Mom . . .

*Fill in the blanks in the following sentences, taking care
not to let the other guests see your answers. When you're done,
hand your answer sheet to the hostess.*

1. My favorite thing about babies is ....

   ....

2. If my baby woke me up four times every night, I would ....

   ....

3. The first solid food I would feed my baby is ....

4. My baby's first word would probably be ....

5. If I needed a break from caring for the baby, I would call ....

6. My ideal number of children would be ....

7. The one thing I would always do for my baby is ....

   ....

8. The one thing I would never do to my baby is ....

   ....

9. The problem with today's parents is ....

   ....

10. When I was a baby I, ...

    ....

If I Were a Mom . . .

Fill in the blanks in the following sentences, taking care not to let the other guests see your answers. When you're done, hand your answer sheet to the hostess.

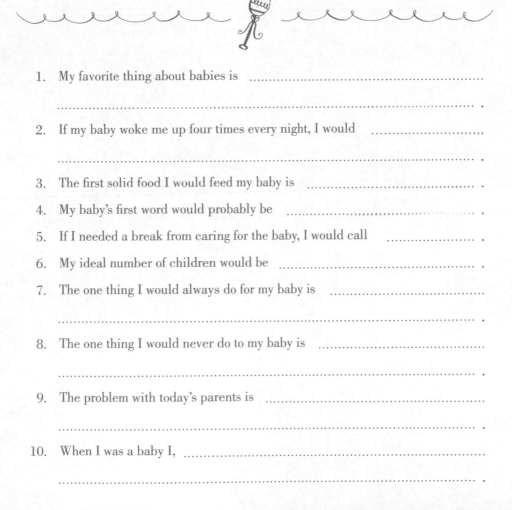

1. My favorite thing about babies is ....

....

2. If my baby woke me up four times every night, I would ....

....

3. The first solid food I would feed my baby is ....

4. My baby's first word would probably be ....

5. If I needed a break from caring for the baby, I would call ....

6. My ideal number of children would be ....

7. The one thing I would always do for my baby is ....

....

8. The one thing I would never do to my baby is ....

....

9. The problem with today's parents is ....

....

10. When I was a baby I, ...

....

If I Were a Mom . . .

*Fill in the blanks in the following sentences, taking care
not to let the other guests see your answers. When you're done,
hand your answer sheet to the hostess.*

1. My favorite thing about babies is ....
    ....

2. If my baby woke me up four times every night, I would ....
    ....

3. The first solid food I would feed my baby is ....

4. My baby's first word would probably be ....

5. If I needed a break from caring for the baby, I would call ....

6. My ideal number of children would be ....

7. The one thing I would always do for my baby is ....
    ....

8. The one thing I would never do to my baby is ....
    ....

9. The problem with today's parents is ....
    ....

10. When I was a baby I, ...
    ....

If I Were a Mom . . .

*Fill in the blanks in the following sentences, taking care
not to let the other guests see your answers. When you're done,
hand your answer sheet to the hostess.*

1. My favorite thing about babies is ....

   ....

2. If my baby woke me up four times every night, I would ....

   ....

3. The first solid food I would feed my baby is ....

4. My baby's first word would probably be ....

5. If I needed a break from caring for the baby, I would call ....

6. My ideal number of children would be ....

7. The one thing I would always do for my baby is ....

   ....

8. The one thing I would never do to my baby is ....

   ....

9. The problem with today's parents is ....

   ....

10. When I was a baby I, ...

    ....

If I Were a Mom . . .

*Fill in the blanks in the following sentences, taking care
not to let the other guests see your answers. When you're done,
hand your answer sheet to the hostess.*

1. My favorite thing about babies is ....
   ....

2. If my baby woke me up four times every night, I would ....
   ....

3. The first solid food I would feed my baby is ....

4. My baby's first word would probably be ....

5. If I needed a break from caring for the baby, I would call ....

6. My ideal number of children would be ....

7. The one thing I would always do for my baby is ....
   ....

8. The one thing I would never do to my baby is ....
   ....

9. The problem with today's parents is ....
   ....

10. When I was a baby I, ...
    ....

Mystery Meats and Other Baby Foods

Each numbered jar contains a different type of baby food.
Taste each one and identify the food in the space provided.

1. ....

2. ....

3. ....

4. ....

5. ....

6. ....

7. ....

8. ....

9. ....

10. ....

name   *score*

Mystery Meats and Other Baby Foods

Each numbered jar contains a different type of baby food.
Taste each one and identify the food in the space provided.

1. ....

2. ....

3. ....

4. ....

5. ....

6. ....

7. ....

8. ....

9. ....

10. ....

name

score

Mystery Meats and
Other Baby Foods

Each numbered jar contains a different type of baby food.
Taste each one and identify the food in the space provided.

1. ....

2. ....

3. ....

4. ....

5. ....

6. ....

7. ....

8. ....

9. ....

10. ....

name   *score*

Mystery Meats and
Other Baby Foods

Each numbered jar contains a different type of baby food.
Taste each one and identify the food in the space provided.

1. ....

2. ....

3. ....

4. ....

5. ....

6. ....

7. ....

8. ....

9. ....

10. ....

name   *score*

Mystery Meats and Other Baby Foods

Each numbered jar contains a different type of baby food.
Taste each one and identify the food in the space provided.

1. ....

2. ....

3. ....

4. ....

5. ....

6. ....

7. ....

8. ....

9. ....

10. ....

name *score*

Mystery Meats and
Other Baby Foods

Each numbered jar contains a different type of baby food.
Taste each one and identify the food in the space provided.

1. ....

2. ....

3. ....

4. ....

5. ....

6. ....

7. ....

8. ....

9. ....

10. ....

name   *score*

Baby
Shower
Games

blocks

diaper pins

rattle

presents

Baby
Shower
Games

No 1

blocks

baby carriage

Mystery Meats and Other Baby Foods

Each numbered jar contains a different type of baby food.
Taste each one and identify the food in the space provided.

1. ....

2. ....

3. ....

4. ....

5. ....

6. ....

7. ....

8. ....

9. ....

10. ....

name

score

It's All Relative

Fill in each blank with the baby's relation, assuming that all parents are married, and have been married only once. Each correct answer is worth 1 point except for the bonus question, which is worth 5. You have two minutes to complete.

1. Baby's sister's son ....

2. Baby's cousin's father ....

3. Baby's mother's mother's mother ....

4. Baby's uncle's wife ....

5. Baby's sister's father's wife ....

6. Baby's father's brother's mother ....

7. Baby's mother's mother's sister ....

8. Baby's sister's uncle's son ....

9. Baby's grandmother's brother's brother ....

10. Baby's brother's son's father ....

11. Baby's mother's mother's sister's sister ....

BONUS *(worth 5 points):*

∗   Baby's grandmother's brother's grandson ....

name   *score*

It's All Relative

Fill in each blank with the baby's relation, assuming that all parents are married, and have been married only once. Each correct answer is worth 1 point except for the bonus question, which is worth 5. You have two minutes to complete.

1. Baby's sister's son ....
2. Baby's cousin's father ....
3. Baby's mother's mother's mother ....
4. Baby's uncle's wife ....
5. Baby's sister's father's wife ....
6. Baby's father's brother's mother ....
7. Baby's mother's mother's sister ....
8. Baby's sister's uncle's son ....
9. Baby's grandmother's brother's brother ....
10. Baby's brother's son's father ....
11. Baby's mother's mother's sister's sister ....

BONUS *(worth 5 points):*

* Baby's grandmother's brother's grandson ....

name   *score*

It's All Relative

Fill in each blank with the baby's relation, assuming that all parents are married, and have been married only once. Each correct answer is worth 1 point except for the bonus question, which is worth 5. You have two minutes to complete.

1. Baby's sister's son ....

2. Baby's cousin's father ....

3. Baby's mother's mother's mother ....

4. Baby's uncle's wife ....

5. Baby's sister's father's wife ....

6. Baby's father's brother's mother ....

7. Baby's mother's mother's sister ....

8. Baby's sister's uncle's son ....

9. Baby's grandmother's brother's brother ....

10. Baby's brother's son's father ....

11. Baby's mother's mother's sister's sister ....

BONUS *(worth 5 points):*

✴ Baby's grandmother's brother's grandson ....

name   *score*

It's All Relative

Fill in each blank with the baby's relation, assuming that all parents are married, and have been married only once. Each correct answer is worth 1 point except for the bonus question, which is worth 5. You have two minutes to complete.

1. Baby's sister's son ....

2. Baby's cousin's father ....

3. Baby's mother's mother's mother ....

4. Baby's uncle's wife ....

5. Baby's sister's father's wife ....

6. Baby's father's brother's mother ....

7. Baby's mother's mother's sister ....

8. Baby's sister's uncle's son ....

9. Baby's grandmother's brother's brother ....

10. Baby's brother's son's father ....

11. Baby's mother's mother's sister's sister ....

BONUS *(worth 5 points):*

✳ Baby's grandmother's brother's grandson ....

name   *score*

It's All Relative

*Fill in each blank with the baby's relation, assuming that all parents
are married, and have been married only once. Each correct answer
is worth 1 point except for the bonus question, which is worth 5.
You have two minutes to complete.*

1. Baby's sister's son ....

2. Baby's cousin's father ....

3. Baby's mother's mother's mother ....

4. Baby's uncle's wife ....

5. Baby's sister's father's wife ....

6. Baby's father's brother's mother ....

7. Baby's mother's mother's sister ....

8. Baby's sister's uncle's son ....

9. Baby's grandmother's brother's brother ....

10. Baby's brother's son's father ....

11. Baby's mother's mother's sister's sister ....

BONUS *(worth 5 points):*

✳ Baby's grandmother's brother's grandson ....

name   *score*

It's All Relative

Fill in each blank with the baby's relation, assuming that all parents
are married, and have been married only once. Each correct answer
is worth 1 point except for the bonus question, which is worth 5.
You have two minutes to complete.

1. Baby's sister's son ....

2. Baby's cousin's father ....

3. Baby's mother's mother's mother ....

4. Baby's uncle's wife ....

5. Baby's sister's father's wife ....

6. Baby's father's brother's mother ....

7. Baby's mother's mother's sister ....

8. Baby's sister's uncle's son ....

9. Baby's grandmother's brother's brother ....

10. Baby's brother's son's father ....

11. Baby's mother's mother's sister's sister ....

BONUS *(worth 5 points):*

✳ Baby's grandmother's brother's grandson ....

name   *score*

It's All Relative

*Fill in each blank with the baby's relation, assuming that all parents
are married, and have been married only once. Each correct answer
is worth 1 point except for the bonus question, which is worth 5.
You have two minutes to complete.*

1.   Baby's sister's son ....

2.   Baby's cousin's father ....

3.   Baby's mother's mother's mother ....

4.   Baby's uncle's wife ....

5.   Baby's sister's father's wife ....

6.   Baby's father's brother's mother ....

7.   Baby's mother's mother's sister ....

8.   Baby's sister's uncle's son ....

9.   Baby's grandmother's brother's brother ....

10. Baby's brother's son's father ....

11. Baby's mother's mother's sister's sister ....

   BONUS *(worth 5 points):*

✳   Baby's grandmother's brother's grandson ....

name   *score*

It's All Relative

*Fill in each blank with the baby's relation, assuming that all parents
are married, and have been married only once. Each correct answer
is worth 1 point except for the bonus question, which is worth 5.
You have two minutes to complete.*

1. Baby's sister's son ....

2. Baby's cousin's father ....

3. Baby's mother's mother's mother ....

4. Baby's uncle's wife ....

5. Baby's sister's father's wife ....

6. Baby's father's brother's mother ....

7. Baby's mother's mother's sister ....

8. Baby's sister's uncle's son ....

9. Baby's grandmother's brother's brother ....

10. Baby's brother's son's father ....

11. Baby's mother's mother's sister's sister ....

BONUS *(worth 5 points):*

✳ Baby's grandmother's brother's grandson ....

name

score

It's All Relative

*Fill in each blank with the baby's relation, assuming that all parents
are married, and have been married only once. Each correct answer
is worth 1 point except for the bonus question, which is worth 5.
You have two minutes to complete.*

1. Baby's sister's son ....
2. Baby's cousin's father ....
3. Baby's mother's mother's mother ....
4. Baby's uncle's wife ....
5. Baby's sister's father's wife ....
6. Baby's father's brother's mother ....
7. Baby's mother's mother's sister ....
8. Baby's sister's uncle's son ....
9. Baby's grandmother's brother's brother ....
10. Baby's brother's son's father ....
11. Baby's mother's mother's sister's sister ....

BONUS *(worth 5 points):*

✱ Baby's grandmother's brother's grandson ....

name   *score*

It's All Relative

*Fill in each blank with the baby's relation, assuming that all parents
are married, and have been married only once. Each correct answer
is worth 1 point except for the bonus question, which is worth 5.
You have two minutes to complete.*

1. Baby's sister's son ....

2. Baby's cousin's father ....

3. Baby's mother's mother's mother ....

4. Baby's uncle's wife ....

5. Baby's sister's father's wife ....

6. Baby's father's brother's mother ....

7. Baby's mother's mother's sister ....

8. Baby's sister's uncle's son ....

9. Baby's grandmother's brother's brother ....

10. Baby's brother's son's father ....

11. Baby's mother's mother's sister's sister ....

BONUS *(worth 5 points):*

✱   Baby's grandmother's brother's grandson ....

name   *score*

TV Tots

For each of the TV youngsters listed below, write the name of the children's show on which he or she appears. You have two minutes to complete.

TV Tot   **TV Show**

1. Pebbles ....
2. Roo ....
3. Bubbles ....
4. Elmo ....
5. Baby Bop ....
6. Baby Kate ....
7. Elroy ....
8. Dilly ....
9. Tinky Winky ....
10. Henrietta Pussycat ....
11. Pikachu ....
12. Mr. Moose ....
13. Spritle ....
14. Boo-Boo Bear ....

name   *score*

TV Tots

For each of the TV youngsters listed below, write the name of the children's show on which he or she appears. You have two minutes to complete.

TV Tot	TV Show
1. Pebbles	....
2. Roo	....
3. Bubbles	....
4. Elmo	....
5. Baby Bop	....
6. Baby Kate	....
7. Elroy	....
8. Dilly	....
9. Tinky Winky	....
10. Henrietta Pussycat	....
11. Pikachu	....
12. Mr. Moose	....
13. Spritle	....
14. Boo-Boo Bear	....

name

score

TV Tots

For each of the TV youngsters listed below, write the name of the children's show on which he or she appears. You have two minutes to complete.

	TV Tot	TV Show
1.	Pebbles	
2.	Roo	
3.	Bubbles	
4.	Elmo	
5.	Baby Bop	
6.	Baby Kate	
7.	Elroy	
8.	Dilly	
9.	Tinky Winky	
10.	Henrietta Pussycat	
11.	Pikachu	
12.	Mr. Moose	
13.	Spritle	
14.	Boo-Boo Bear	

name

score

TV Tots

For each of the TV youngsters listed below, write the name of the children's show on which he or she appears. You have two minutes to complete.

	TV Tot	TV Show
1.	Pebbles	....
2.	Roo	....
3.	Bubbles	....
4.	Elmo	....
5.	Baby Bop	....
6.	Baby Kate	....
7.	Elroy	....
8.	Dilly	....
9.	Tinky Winky	....
10.	Henrietta Pussycat	....
11.	Pikachu	....
12.	Mr. Moose	....
13.	Spritle	....
14.	Boo-Boo Bear	....

name

score

TV Tots

For each of the TV youngsters listed below, write the name of the children's show on which he or she appears. You have two minutes to complete.

TV Tot	TV Show
1. Pebbles	....
2. Roo	....
3. Bubbles	....
4. Elmo	....
5. Baby Bop	....
6. Baby Kate	....
7. Elroy	....
8. Dilly	....
9. Tinky Winky	....
10. Henrietta Pussycat	....
11. Pikachu	....
12. Mr. Moose	....
13. Spritle	....
14. Boo-Boo Bear	....

name   *score*

TV Tots

For each of the TV youngsters listed below, write the name of the children's show on which he or she appears. You have two minutes to complete.

	TV Tot	*TV Show*
1.	Pebbles	
2.	Roo	
3.	Bubbles	
4.	Elmo	
5.	Baby Bop	
6.	Baby Kate	
7.	Elroy	
8.	Dilly	
9.	Tinky Winky	
10.	Henrietta Pussycat	
11.	Pikachu	
12.	Mr. Moose	
13.	Spritle	
14.	Boo-Boo Bear	

name   *score*

TV Tots

For each of the TV youngsters listed below, write the name of the children's show on which he or she appears. You have two minutes to complete.

	TV Tot	**TV Show**
1.	Pebbles	....
2.	Roo	....
3.	Bubbles	....
4.	Elmo	....
5.	Baby Bop	....
6.	Baby Kate	....
7.	Elroy	....
8.	Dilly	....
9.	Tinky Winky	....
10.	Henrietta Pussycat	....
11.	Pikachu	....
12.	Mr. Moose	....
13.	Spritle	....
14.	Boo-Boo Bear	....

name *score*

TV Tots

For each of the TV youngsters listed below, write the name of the children's show on which he or she appears. You have two minutes to complete.

TV Tot	TV Show
1. Pebbles	....
2. Roo	....
3. Bubbles	....
4. Elmo	....
5. Baby Bop	....
6. Baby Kate	....
7. Elroy	....
8. Dilly	....
9. Tinky Winky	....
10. Henrietta Pussycat	....
11. Pikachu	....
12. Mr. Moose	....
13. Spritle	....
14. Boo-Boo Bear	....

name

score

TV Tots

For each of the TV youngsters listed below, write the name of the children's show on which he or she appears. You have two minutes to complete.

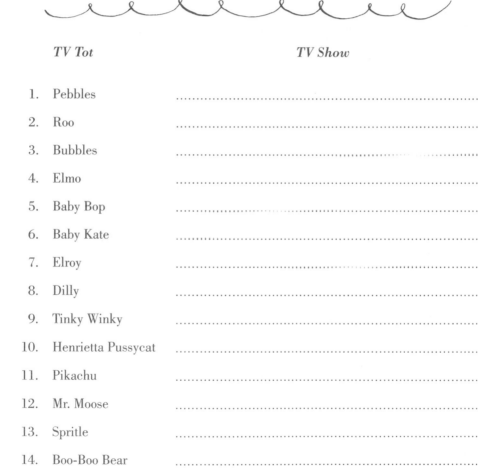

	TV Tot	TV Show
1.	Pebbles	....
2.	Roo	....
3.	Bubbles	....
4.	Elmo	....
5.	Baby Bop	....
6.	Baby Kate	....
7.	Elroy	....
8.	Dilly	....
9.	Tinky Winky	....
10.	Henrietta Pussycat	....
11.	Pikachu	....
12.	Mr. Moose	....
13.	Spritle	....
14.	Boo-Boo Bear	....

name

score

Animal Babies

For each of the following animals, fill in the blank with the name of its baby.
You have two minutes to complete.

	Animal	Baby		Animal	Baby
1.	Goat	....	9.	Penguin	....
2.	Cow	....	10.	Swan	....
3.	Bear	....	11.	Kangaroo	....
4.	Deer	....	12.	Horse	....
5.	Goose	....	13.	Owl	....
6.	Sheep	....	14.	Camel	....
7.	Elephant	....	15.	Alligator	....
8.	Seal	....	16.	Fish	....

name   *score*

Animal Babies

For each of the following animals, fill in the blank with the name of its baby.
You have two minutes to complete.

	Animal	Baby		Animal	Baby
1.	Goat	....	9.	Penguin	....
2.	Cow	....	10.	Swan	....
3.	Bear	....	11.	Kangaroo	....
4.	Deer	....	12.	Horse	....
5.	Goose	....	13.	Owl	....
6.	Sheep	....	14.	Camel	....
7.	Elephant	....	15.	Alligator	....
8.	Seal	....	16.	Fish	....

name   *score*

Animal Babies

For each of the following animals, fill in the blank with the name of its baby.
You have two minutes to complete.

Animal	Baby		Animal	Baby
1. Goat	....		9. Penguin	....
2. Cow	....		10. Swan	....
3. Bear	....		11. Kangaroo	....
4. Deer	....		12. Horse	....
5. Goose	....		13. Owl	....
6. Sheep	....		14. Camel	....
7. Elephant	....		15. Alligator	....
8. Seal	....		16. Fish	....

name   *score*

Animal Babies

For each of the following animals, fill in the blank with the name of its baby.
You have two minutes to complete.

	Animal	Baby		Animal	Baby
1.	Goat	....	9.	Penguin	....
2.	Cow	....	10.	Swan	....
3.	Bear	....	11.	Kangaroo	....
4.	Deer	....	12.	Horse	....
5.	Goose	....	13.	Owl	....
6.	Sheep	....	14.	Camel	....
7.	Elephant	....	15.	Alligator	....
8.	Seal	....	16.	Fish	....

name *score*

Animal Babies

For each of the following animals, fill in the blank with the name of its baby.
You have two minutes to complete.

	Animal	*Baby*		*Animal*	*Baby*
1.	Goat	....	9.	Penguin	....
2.	Cow	....	10.	Swan	....
3.	Bear	....	11.	Kangaroo	....
4.	Deer	....	12.	Horse	....
5.	Goose	....	13.	Owl	....
6.	Sheep	....	14.	Camel	....
7.	Elephant	....	15.	Alligator	....
8.	Seal	....	16.	Fish	....

name   *score*

Animal Babies

For each of the following animals, fill in the blank with the name of its baby.
You have two minutes to complete.

	Animal	Baby		Animal	Baby
1.	Goat	....	9.	Penguin	....
2.	Cow	....	10.	Swan	....
3.	Bear	....	11.	Kangaroo	....
4.	Deer	....	12.	Horse	....
5.	Goose	....	13.	Owl	....
6.	Sheep	....	14.	Camel	....
7.	Elephant	....	15.	Alligator	....
8.	Seal	....	16.	Fish	....

name   *score*

Animal Babies

For each of the following animals, fill in the blank with the name of its baby.
You have two minutes to complete.

	Animal	Baby		Animal	Baby
1.	Goat	....	9.	Penguin	....
2.	Cow	....	10.	Swan	....
3.	Bear	....	11.	Kangaroo	....
4.	Deer	....	12.	Horse	....
5.	Goose	....	13.	Owl	....
6.	Sheep	....	14.	Camel	....
7.	Elephant	....	15.	Alligator	....
8.	Seal	....	16.	Fish	....

name   *score*

Animal Babies

For each of the following animals, fill in the blank with the name of its baby.
You have two minutes to complete.

	Animal	Baby			Animal	Baby
1.	Goat	....		9.	Penguin	....
2.	Cow	....		10.	Swan	....
3.	Bear	....		11.	Kangaroo	....
4.	Deer	....		12.	Horse	....
5.	Goose	....		13.	Owl	....
6.	Sheep	....		14.	Camel	....
7.	Elephant	....		15.	Alligator	....
8.	Seal	....		16.	Fish	....

name   score

Animal Babies

For each of the following animals, fill in the blank with the name of its baby.
You have two minutes to complete.

	Animal	*Baby*		*Animal*	*Baby*
1.	Goat	....	9.	Penguin	....
2.	Cow	....	10.	Swan	....
3.	Bear	....	11.	Kangaroo	....
4.	Deer	....	12.	Horse	....
5.	Goose	....	13.	Owl	....
6.	Sheep	....	14.	Camel	....
7.	Elephant	....	15.	Alligator	....
8.	Seal	....	16.	Fish	....

name *score*

Animal Babies

For each of the following animals, fill in the blank with the name of its baby.
You have two minutes to complete.

	Animal	*Baby*		*Animal*	*Baby*
1.	Goat	....	9.	Penguin	....
2.	Cow	....	10.	Swan	....
3.	Bear	....	11.	Kangaroo	....
4.	Deer	....	12.	Horse	....
5.	Goose	....	13.	Owl	....
6.	Sheep	....	14.	Camel	....
7.	Elephant	....	15.	Alligator	....
8.	Seal	....	16.	Fish	....

name   *score*

Baby Shower Games
blocks
diaper pins
rattle
presents
Baby Shower Games
No. 1
blocks
baby carriage

Animal Babies

For each of the following animals, fill in the blank with the name of its baby.
You have two minutes to complete.

Animal	Baby		Animal	Baby
1. Goat	....		9. Penguin	....
2. Cow	....		10. Swan	....
3. Bear	....		11. Kangaroo	....
4. Deer	....		12. Horse	....
5. Goose	....		13. Owl	....
6. Sheep	....		14. Camel	....
7. Elephant	....		15. Alligator	....
8. Seal	....		16. Fish	....

name *score*

Animal Babies

For each of the following animals, fill in the blank with the name of its baby.
You have two minutes to complete.

	Animal	*Baby*		*Animal*	*Baby*
1.	Goat	....	9.	Penguin	....
2.	Cow	....	10.	Swan	....
3.	Bear	....	11.	Kangaroo	....
4.	Deer	....	12.	Horse	....
5.	Goose	....	13.	Owl	....
6.	Sheep	....	14.	Camel	....
7.	Elephant	....	15.	Alligator	....
8.	Seal	....	16.	Fish	....

name *score*

Animal Babies

For each of the following animals, fill in the blank with the name of its baby. You have two minutes to complete.

	Animal	Baby		Animal	Baby
1.	Goat	....	9.	Penguin	....
2.	Cow	....	10.	Swan	....
3.	Bear	....	11.	Kangaroo	....
4.	Deer	....	12.	Horse	....
5.	Goose	....	13.	Owl	....
6.	Sheep	....	14.	Camel	....
7.	Elephant	....	15.	Alligator	....
8.	Seal	....	16.	Fish	....

name   *score*

Animal Babies

For each of the following animals, fill in the blank with the name of its baby.
You have two minutes to complete.

	Animal	*Baby*		*Animal*	*Baby*
1.	Goat	....	9.	Penguin	....
2.	Cow	....	10.	Swan	....
3.	Bear	....	11.	Kangaroo	....
4.	Deer	....	12.	Horse	....
5.	Goose	....	13.	Owl	....
6.	Sheep	....	14.	Camel	....
7.	Elephant	....	15.	Alligator	....
8.	Seal	....	16.	Fish	....

name *score*

Animal Babies

For each of the following animals, fill in the blank with the name of its baby.
You have two minutes to complete.

	Animal	Baby		Animal	Baby
1.	Goat	....	9.	Penguin	....
2.	Cow	....	10.	Swan	....
3.	Bear	....	11.	Kangaroo	....
4.	Deer	....	12.	Horse	....
5.	Goose	....	13.	Owl	....
6.	Sheep	....	14.	Camel	....
7.	Elephant	....	15.	Alligator	....
8.	Seal	....	16.	Fish	....

name   *score*

Newborn Know-How

Would you be ready to bring home a baby? Compare your newborn know-how with that of the mom-to-be. You have three minutes to complete.

1. Which of the baby's five senses develops first?...

2. How many hours a day does the average newborn sleep?
   a. 16 hours   *b.* 13 hours   *c.* 18 hours   *d.* 15 hours

3. What was the age of the oldest woman in the world to give birth?
   a. 62   *b.* 59   *c.* 64   *d.* 67

4. When inventing the precursor to the modern disposable diaper in the 1940s, Marion Donovan used what household item to make a reusable waterproof diaper cover?
   a. A swimming cap   *b.* A shower curtain   *c.* A hot water bottle   *d.* Rubber gloves

5. Newborn breastfeeding babies are likely to get hungry how often?..........................

6. According to the Social Security Administration, what was the most popular name for baby boys and baby girls in the U.S. in the year 1900?
   a. Michael and Elizabeth   *b.* Theodore and Margaret
   c. John and Mary   *d.* Edward and Victoria

7. According to the Social Security Administration, what was the most popular name for baby boys and baby girls in the U.S. in the year 2000?
   a. Jacob and Emily   *b.* Caitlin and Joshua
   c. Matthew and Hannah   *d.* Michael and Erin

8. About how many diapers do most newborns wet every day?
   a. 11–15   *b.* 7–9   *c.* 8–10   *d.* 5–7

9. The MMR vaccine that most children receive at about one year of age protects against which three diseases?...

10. In what year was the first "test-tube baby" born?
    a. 1971   *b.* 1978   *c.* 1982   *d.* 1969

name   *score*

Newborn Know-How

Would you be ready to bring home a baby? Compare your newborn know-how with that of the mom-to-be. You have three minutes to complete.

1. Which of the baby's five senses develops first?...

2. How many hours a day does the average newborn sleep?
    a. 16 hours　*b.* 13 hours　*c.* 18 hours　*d.* 15 hours

3. What was the age of the oldest woman in the world to give birth?
    a. 62　*b.* 59　*c.* 64　*d.* 67

4. When inventing the precursor to the modern disposable diaper in the 1940s, Marion Donovan used what household item to make a reusable waterproof diaper cover?
    a. A swimming cap　*b.* A shower curtain　*c.* A hot water bottle　*d.* Rubber gloves

5. Newborn breastfeeding babies are likely to get hungry how often?...........................

6. According to the Social Security Administration, what was the most popular name for baby boys and baby girls in the U.S. in the year 1900?
    a. Michael and Elizabeth　　　　*b.* Theodore and Margaret
    c. John and Mary　　　　　　　*d.* Edward and Victoria

7. According to the Social Security Administration, what was the most popular name for baby boys and baby girls in the U.S. in the year 2000?
    a. Jacob and Emily　　　　　　*b.* Caitlin and Joshua
    c. Matthew and Hannah　　　　*d.* Michael and Erin

8. About how many diapers do most newborns wet every day?
    a. 11–15　*b.* 7–9　*c.* 8–10　*d.* 5–7

9. The MMR vaccine that most children receive at about one year of age protects against which three diseases?...

10. In what year was the first "test-tube baby" born?
    a. 1971　*b.* 1978　*c.* 1982　*d.* 1969

name　　　　　　　　　　　　　　　　　　　score

Newborn Know-How

Would you be ready to bring home a baby? Compare your newborn know-how with that of the mom-to-be. You have three minutes to complete.

1. Which of the baby's five senses develops first?..

2. How many hours a day does the average newborn sleep?
   a. 16 hours   *b.* 13 hours   *c.* 18 hours   *d.* 15 hours

3. What was the age of the oldest woman in the world to give birth?
   a. 62   *b.* 59   *c.* 64   *d.* 67

4. When inventing the precursor to the modern disposable diaper in the 1940s, Marion Donovan used what household item to make a reusable waterproof diaper cover?
   a. A swimming cap   *b.* A shower curtain   *c.* A hot water bottle   *d.* Rubber gloves

5. Newborn breastfeeding babies are likely to get hungry how often?..........................

6. According to the Social Security Administration, what was the most popular name for baby boys and baby girls in the U.S. in the year 1900?
   a. Michael and Elizabeth   *b.* Theodore and Margaret
   c. John and Mary   *d.* Edward and Victoria

7. According to the Social Security Administration, what was the most popular name for baby boys and baby girls in the U.S. in the year 2000?
   a. Jacob and Emily   *b.* Caitlin and Joshua
   c. Matthew and Hannah   *d.* Michael and Erin

8. About how many diapers do most newborns wet every day?
   a. 11–15   *b.* 7–9   *c.* 8–10   *d.* 5–7

9. The MMR vaccine that most children receive at about one year of age protects against which three diseases?...

10. In what year was the first "test-tube baby" born?
    a. 1971   *b.* 1978   *c.* 1982   *d.* 1969

name   *score*

Newborn Know-How

Would you be ready to bring home a baby? Compare your newborn know-how with that of the mom-to-be. You have three minutes to complete.

1. Which of the baby's five senses develops first?...

2. How many hours a day does the average newborn sleep?
   a. 16 hours   *b.* 13 hours   *c.* 18 hours   *d.* 15 hours

3. What was the age of the oldest woman in the world to give birth?
   a. 62   *b.* 59   *c.* 64   *d.* 67

4. When inventing the precursor to the modern disposable diaper in the 1940s, Marion Donovan used what household item to make a reusable waterproof diaper cover?
   a. A swimming cap   *b.* A shower curtain   *c.* A hot water bottle   *d.* Rubber gloves

5. Newborn breastfeeding babies are likely to get hungry how often?..........................

6. According to the Social Security Administration, what was the most popular name for baby boys and baby girls in the U.S. in the year 1900?
   a. Michael and Elizabeth   *b.* Theodore and Margaret
   c. John and Mary   *d.* Edward and Victoria

7. According to the Social Security Administration, what was the most popular name for baby boys and baby girls in the U.S. in the year 2000?
   a. Jacob and Emily   *b.* Caitlin and Joshua
   c. Matthew and Hannah   *d.* Michael and Erin

8. About how many diapers do most newborns wet every day?
   a. 11–15   *b.* 7–9   *c.* 8–10   *d.* 5–7

9. The MMR vaccine that most children receive at about one year of age protects against which three diseases?...

10. In what year was the first "test-tube baby" born?
    a. 1971   *b.* 1978   *c.* 1982   *d.* 1969

name

score

Newborn Know-How

Would you be ready to bring home a baby? Compare your newborn know-how with that of the mom-to-be. You have three minutes to complete.

1. Which of the baby's five senses develops first?...

2. How many hours a day does the average newborn sleep?
   a. 16 hours   *b.* 13 hours   *c.* 18 hours   *d.* 15 hours

3. What was the age of the oldest woman in the world to give birth?
   a. 62   *b.* 59   *c.* 64   *d.* 67

4. When inventing the precursor to the modern disposable diaper in the 1940s, Marion Donovan used what household item to make a reusable waterproof diaper cover?
   a. A swimming cap   *b.* A shower curtain   *c.* A hot water bottle   *d.* Rubber gloves

5. Newborn breastfeeding babies are likely to get hungry how often?...........................

6. According to the Social Security Administration, what was the most popular name for baby boys and baby girls in the U.S. in the year 1900?
   a. Michael and Elizabeth   *b.* Theodore and Margaret
   c. John and Mary   *d.* Edward and Victoria

7. According to the Social Security Administration, what was the most popular name for baby boys and baby girls in the U.S. in the year 2000?
   a. Jacob and Emily   *b.* Caitlin and Joshua
   c. Matthew and Hannah   *d.* Michael and Erin

8. About how many diapers do most newborns wet every day?
   a. 11–15   *b.* 7–9   *c.* 8–10   *d.* 5–7

9. The MMR vaccine that most children receive at about one year of age protects against which three diseases?...

10. In what year was the first "test-tube baby" born?
    a. 1971   *b.* 1978   *c.* 1982   *d.* 1969

name

score

Newborn Know-How

Would you be ready to bring home a baby? Compare your newborn know-how with that of the mom-to-be. You have three minutes to complete.

1. Which of the baby's five senses develops first?...

2. How many hours a day does the average newborn sleep?
    a. 16 hours   *b.* 13 hours   *c.* 18 hours   *d.* 15 hours

3. What was the age of the oldest woman in the world to give birth?
    a. 62   *b.* 59   *c.* 64   *d.* 67

4. When inventing the precursor to the modern disposable diaper in the 1940s, Marion Donovan used what household item to make a reusable waterproof diaper cover?
    a. A swimming cap   *b.* A shower curtain   *c.* A hot water bottle   *d.* Rubber gloves

5. Newborn breastfeeding babies are likely to get hungry how often?..........................

6. According to the Social Security Administration, what was the most popular name for baby boys and baby girls in the U.S. in the year 1900?
    a. Michael and Elizabeth   *b.* Theodore and Margaret
    c. John and Mary   *d.* Edward and Victoria

7. According to the Social Security Administration, what was the most popular name for baby boys and baby girls in the U.S. in the year 2000?
    a. Jacob and Emily   *b.* Caitlin and Joshua
    c. Matthew and Hannah   *d.* Michael and Erin

8. About how many diapers do most newborns wet every day?
    a. 11–15   *b.* 7–9   *c.* 8–10   *d.* 5–7

9. The MMR vaccine that most children receive at about one year of age protects against which three diseases?...

10. In what year was the first "test-tube baby" born?
    a. 1971   *b.* 1978   *c.* 1982   *d.* 1969

NAME   score

Newborn Know-How

Would you be ready to bring home a baby? Compare your newborn know-how with that of the mom-to-be. You have three minutes to complete.

1. Which of the baby's five senses develops first?..

2. How many hours a day does the average newborn sleep?
   a. 16 hours   *b.* 13 hours   *c.* 18 hours   *d.* 15 hours

3. What was the age of the oldest woman in the world to give birth?
   a. 62   *b.* 59   *c.* 64   *d.* 67

4. When inventing the precursor to the modern disposable diaper in the 1940s, Marion Donovan used what household item to make a reusable waterproof diaper cover?
   a. A swimming cap   *b.* A shower curtain   *c.* A hot water bottle   *d.* Rubber gloves

5. Newborn breastfeeding babies are likely to get hungry how often?............................

6. According to the Social Security Administration, what was the most popular name for baby boys and baby girls in the U.S. in the year 1900?
   a. Michael and Elizabeth   *b.* Theodore and Margaret
   c. John and Mary   *d.* Edward and Victoria

7. According to the Social Security Administration, what was the most popular name for baby boys and baby girls in the U.S. in the year 2000?
   a. Jacob and Emily   *b.* Caitlin and Joshua
   c. Matthew and Hannah   *d.* Michael and Erin

8. About how many diapers do most newborns wet every day?
   a. 11–15   *b.* 7–9   *c.* 8–10   *d.* 5–7

9. The MMR vaccine that most children receive at about one year of age protects against which three diseases?..

10. In what year was the first "test-tube baby" born?
    a. 1971   *b.* 1978   *c.* 1982   *d.* 1969

name

score

Newborn Know-How

Would you be ready to bring home a baby? Compare your newborn know-how with that of the mom-to-be. You have three minutes to complete.

1. Which of the baby's five senses develops first?...

2. How many hours a day does the average newborn sleep?
   a. 16 hours   *b.* 13 hours   *c.* 18 hours   *d.* 15 hours

3. What was the age of the oldest woman in the world to give birth?
   a. 62   *b.* 59   *c.* 64   *d.* 67

4. When inventing the precursor to the modern disposable diaper in the 1940s, Marion Donovan used what household item to make a reusable waterproof diaper cover?
   a. A swimming cap   *b.* A shower curtain   *c.* A hot water bottle   *d.* Rubber gloves

5. Newborn breastfeeding babies are likely to get hungry how often?...........................

6. According to the Social Security Administration, what was the most popular name for baby boys and baby girls in the U.S. in the year 1900?
   a. Michael and Elizabeth   *b.* Theodore and Margaret
   c. John and Mary   *d.* Edward and Victoria

7. According to the Social Security Administration, what was the most popular name for baby boys and baby girls in the U.S. in the year 2000?
   a. Jacob and Emily   *b.* Caitlin and Joshua
   c. Matthew and Hannah   *d.* Michael and Erin

8. About how many diapers do most newborns wet every day?
   a. 11–15   *b.* 7–9   *c.* 8–10   *d.* 5–7

9. The MMR vaccine that most children receive at about one year of age protects against which three diseases?..

10. In what year was the first "test-tube baby" born?
    a. 1971   *b.* 1978   *c.* 1982   *d.* 1969

name

score

Newborn Know-How

Would you be ready to bring home a baby? Compare your newborn know-how with that of the mom-to-be. You have three minutes to complete.

1. Which of the baby's five senses develops first?..

2. How many hours a day does the average newborn sleep?
   a. 16 hours   *b.* 13 hours   *c.* 18 hours   *d.* 15 hours

3. What was the age of the oldest woman in the world to give birth?
   a. 62   *b.* 59   *c.* 64   *d.* 67

4. When inventing the precursor to the modern disposable diaper in the 1940s, Marion Donovan used what household item to make a reusable waterproof diaper cover?
   a. A swimming cap   *b.* A shower curtain   *c.* A hot water bottle   *d.* Rubber gloves

5. Newborn breastfeeding babies are likely to get hungry how often?..........................

6. According to the Social Security Administration, what was the most popular name for baby boys and baby girls in the U.S. in the year 1900?
   a. Michael and Elizabeth   *b.* Theodore and Margaret
   c. John and Mary   *d.* Edward and Victoria

7. According to the Social Security Administration, what was the most popular name for baby boys and baby girls in the U.S. in the year 2000?
   a. Jacob and Emily   *b.* Caitlin and Joshua
   c. Matthew and Hannah   *d.* Michael and Erin

8. About how many diapers do most newborns wet every day?
   a. 11–15   *b.* 7–9   *c.* 8–10   *d.* 5–7

9. The MMR vaccine that most children receive at about one year of age protects against which three diseases?..

10. In what year was the first "test-tube baby" born?
    a. 1971   *b.* 1978   *c.* 1982   *d.* 1969

name   *score*

Newborn Know-How

Would you be ready to bring home a baby? Compare your newborn know-how
with that of the mom-to-be. You have three minutes to complete.

1. Which of the baby's five senses develops first?...

2. How many hours a day does the average newborn sleep?
   a. 16 hours   *b.* 13 hours   *c.* 18 hours   *d.* 15 hours

3. What was the age of the oldest woman in the world to give birth?
   a. 62   *b.* 59   *c.* 64   *d.* 67

4. When inventing the precursor to the modern disposable diaper in the 1940s, Marion
   Donovan used what household item to make a reusable waterproof diaper cover?
   a. A swimming cap   *b.* A shower curtain   *c.* A hot water bottle   *d.* Rubber gloves

5. Newborn breastfeeding babies are likely to get hungry how often?...........................

6. According to the Social Security Administration, what was the most popular name
   for baby boys and baby girls in the U.S. in the year 1900?
   a. Michael and Elizabeth   *b.* Theodore and Margaret
   c. John and Mary   *d.* Edward and Victoria

7. According to the Social Security Administration, what was the most popular name
   for baby boys and baby girls in the U.S. in the year 2000?
   a. Jacob and Emily   *b.* Caitlin and Joshua
   c. Matthew and Hannah   *d.* Michael and Erin

8. About how many diapers do most newborns wet every day?
   a. 11–15   *b.* 7–9   *c.* 8–10   *d.* 5–7

9. The MMR vaccine that most children receive at about one year of age protects against
   which three diseases?...

10. In what year was the first "test-tube baby" born?
    a. 1971   *b.* 1978   *c.* 1982   *d.* 1969

name   *score*

Newborn Know-How

*Would you be ready to bring home a baby? Compare your newborn know-how
with that of the mom-to-be. You have three minutes to complete.*

1. Which of the baby's five senses develops first?..

2. How many hours a day does the average newborn sleep?
   a. 16 hours   *b.* 13 hours   *c.* 18 hours   *d.* 15 hours

3. What was the age of the oldest woman in the world to give birth?
   a. 62   *b.* 59   *c.* 64   *d.* 67

4. When inventing the precursor to the modern disposable diaper in the 1940s, Marion
   Donovan used what household item to make a reusable waterproof diaper cover?
   a. A swimming cap   *b.* A shower curtain   *c.* A hot water bottle   *d.* Rubber gloves

5. Newborn breastfeeding babies are likely to get hungry how often?...........................

6. According to the Social Security Administration, what was the most popular name
   for baby boys and baby girls in the U.S. in the year 1900?
   a. Michael and Elizabeth   *b.* Theodore and Margaret
   c. John and Mary   *d.* Edward and Victoria

7. According to the Social Security Administration, what was the most popular name
   for baby boys and baby girls in the U.S. in the year 2000?
   a. Jacob and Emily   *b.* Caitlin and Joshua
   c. Matthew and Hannah   *d.* Michael and Erin

8. About how many diapers do most newborns wet every day?
   a. 11–15   *b.* 7–9   *c.* 8–10   *d.* 5–7

9. The MMR vaccine that most children receive at about one year of age protects against
   which three diseases?..

10. In what year was the first "test-tube baby" born?
    a. 1971   *b.* 1978   *c.* 1982   *d.* 1969

name   *score*

Newborn Know-How

Would you be ready to bring home a baby? Compare your newborn know-how
with that of the mom-to-be. You have three minutes to complete.

1. Which of the baby's five senses develops first?...

2. How many hours a day does the average newborn sleep?
    a. 16 hours   *b.* 13 hours   *c.* 18 hours   *d.* 15 hours

3. What was the age of the oldest woman in the world to give birth?
    a. 62   *b.* 59   *c.* 64   *d.* 67

4. When inventing the precursor to the modern disposable diaper in the 1940s, Marion
    Donovan used what household item to make a reusable waterproof diaper cover?
    a. A swimming cap   *b.* A shower curtain   *c.* A hot water bottle   *d.* Rubber gloves

5. Newborn breastfeeding babies are likely to get hungry how often?..........................

6. According to the Social Security Administration, what was the most popular name
    for baby boys and baby girls in the U.S. in the year 1900?
    a. Michael and Elizabeth   *b.* Theodore and Margaret
    c. John and Mary   *d.* Edward and Victoria

7. According to the Social Security Administration, what was the most popular name
    for baby boys and baby girls in the U.S. in the year 2000?
    a. Jacob and Emily   *b.* Caitlin and Joshua
    c. Matthew and Hannah   *d.* Michael and Erin

8. About how many diapers do most newborns wet every day?
    a. 11–15   *b.* 7–9   *c.* 8–10   *d.* 5–7

9. The MMR vaccine that most children receive at about one year of age protects against
    which three diseases?...

10. In what year was the first "test-tube baby" born?
    a. 1971   *b.* 1978   *c.* 1982   *d.* 1969

name   *score*

Newborn Know-How

Would you be ready to bring home a baby? Compare your newborn know-how
with that of the mom-to-be. You have three minutes to complete.

1. Which of the baby's five senses develops first?..

2. How many hours a day does the average newborn sleep?
    a. 16 hours   *b.* 13 hours   *c.* 18 hours   *d.* 15 hours

3. What was the age of the oldest woman in the world to give birth?
    a. 62   *b.* 59   *c.* 64   *d.* 67

4. When inventing the precursor to the modern disposable diaper in the 1940s, Marion
    Donovan used what household item to make a reusable waterproof diaper cover?
    a. A swimming cap   *b.* A shower curtain   *c.* A hot water bottle   *d.* Rubber gloves

5. Newborn breastfeeding babies are likely to get hungry how often?..........................

6. According to the Social Security Administration, what was the most popular name
    for baby boys and baby girls in the U.S. in the year 1900?
    a. Michael and Elizabeth   *b.* Theodore and Margaret
    c. John and Mary   *d.* Edward and Victoria

7. According to the Social Security Administration, what was the most popular name
    for baby boys and baby girls in the U.S. in the year 2000?
    a. Jacob and Emily   *b.* Caitlin and Joshua
    c. Matthew and Hannah   *d.* Michael and Erin

8. About how many diapers do most newborns wet every day?
    a. 11–15   *b.* 7–9   *c.* 8–10   *d.* 5–7

9. The MMR vaccine that most children receive at about one year of age protects against
    which three diseases?...

10. In what year was the first "test-tube baby" born?
    a. 1971   *b.* 1978   *c.* 1982   *d.* 1969

name   *score*

Newborn Know-How

Would you be ready to bring home a baby? Compare your newborn know-how with that of the mom-to-be. You have three minutes to complete.

1. Which of the baby's five senses develops first?...

2. How many hours a day does the average newborn sleep?
    a. 16 hours   *b.* 13 hours   *c.* 18 hours   *d.* 15 hours

3. What was the age of the oldest woman in the world to give birth?
    a. 62   *b.* 59   *c.* 64   *d.* 67

4. When inventing the precursor to the modern disposable diaper in the 1940s, Marion Donovan used what household item to make a reusable waterproof diaper cover?
    a. A swimming cap   *b.* A shower curtain   *c.* A hot water bottle   *d.* Rubber gloves

5. Newborn breastfeeding babies are likely to get hungry how often?...........................

6. According to the Social Security Administration, what was the most popular name for baby boys and baby girls in the U.S. in the year 1900?
    a. Michael and Elizabeth   *b.* Theodore and Margaret
    c. John and Mary   *d.* Edward and Victoria

7. According to the Social Security Administration, what was the most popular name for baby boys and baby girls in the U.S. in the year 2000?
    a. Jacob and Emily   *b.* Caitlin and Joshua
    c. Matthew and Hannah   *d.* Michael and Erin

8. About how many diapers do most newborns wet every day?
    a. 11–15   *b.* 7–9   *c.* 8–10   *d.* 5–7

9. The MMR vaccine that most children receive at about one year of age protects against which three diseases?...

10. In what year was the first "test-tube baby" born?
    a. 1971   *b.* 1978   *c.* 1982   *d.* 1969

name   *score*

Newborn Know-How

Would you be ready to bring home a baby? Compare your newborn know-how with that of the mom-to-be. You have three minutes to complete.

1. Which of the baby's five senses develops first?..

2. How many hours a day does the average newborn sleep?
   a. 16 hours   *b.* 13 hours   *c.* 18 hours   *d.* 15 hours

3. What was the age of the oldest woman in the world to give birth?
   a. 62   *b.* 59   *c.* 64   *d.* 67

4. When inventing the precursor to the modern disposable diaper in the 1940s, Marion Donovan used what household item to make a reusable waterproof diaper cover?
   a. A swimming cap   *b.* A shower curtain   *c.* A hot water bottle   *d.* Rubber gloves

5. Newborn breastfeeding babies are likely to get hungry how often?..........................

6. According to the Social Security Administration, what was the most popular name for baby boys and baby girls in the U.S. in the year 1900?
   a. Michael and Elizabeth   *b.* Theodore and Margaret
   c. John and Mary   *d.* Edward and Victoria

7. According to the Social Security Administration, what was the most popular name for baby boys and baby girls in the U.S. in the year 2000?
   a. Jacob and Emily   *b.* Caitlin and Joshua
   c. Matthew and Hannah   *d.* Michael and Erin

8. About how many diapers do most newborns wet every day?
   a. 11–15   *b.* 7–9   *c.* 8–10   *d.* 5–7

9. The MMR vaccine that most children receive at about one year of age protects against which three diseases?...

10. In what year was the first "test-tube baby" born?
    a. 1971   *b.* 1978   *c.* 1982   *d.* 1969

name

score

Gift Tracker

from	gift	Thank-you sent
....	....	⚬
....	....	⚬
....	....	⚬
....	....	⚬
....	....	⚬
....	....	⚬
....	....	⚬
....	....	⚬
....	....	⚬
....	....	⚬

Gift Tracker

from	*gift*	Thank-you sent
		○
		○
		○
		○
		○
		○
		○
		○
		○
		○
		○